Reduce, Reuse

Sally Hewitt

W
FRANKLIN WATTS
LONDON • SYDNEY

This edition 2011
First published in 2008 by
Franklin Watts
338 Euston Road
London NW1 3BH

Franklin Watts Australia
Level 17/207 Kent Street
Sydney NSW 2000
Copyright © Franklin Watts 2008

Editor: Jeremy Smith
Design: Jason Anscomb
All rights reserved.
A CIP catalogue record for this book
is available from the British Library.

Picture credits: Alamy: 6, 7b, 8, 10 all, 11 all, 18 all, 19, 21tr, 22 all,
23 all, 24. Corbis: 14. Computers for Schools: 17b. Freecycle: 9b & t. Friends of Malawi
Orphans: 15 all. istockphoto: 21tl. Shutterstock: OFC, 3, 7t, 9r, 12, 16, 17t. St Joseph's
School: 13 all. Trafalgar Infant & Junior School: 26-27 all. Wonga Beach School: 20 all.

Every attempt has been made to clear copyright. Should there be any inadvertent
omission, please contact the publisher for rectification.

Dewey Classification: 941.085

ISBN: 978 1 4451 0598 7

Printed in China

Franklin Watts is a division of Hachette Children's Books,
an Hachette UK company
www.hachette.co.uk.

Contents

Going to waste

Natural resources such as wood, metals, oil and gas are used to make all kinds of things we use every day. We often throw these things away without a thought, creating waste that ends up in a variety of different places.

We all produce a vast amount of rubbish every year. Landfill sites like the one above will rapidly fill up unless we start reducing the amount we throw away.

Where does it go?

Litter

Some waste is thrown carelessly and lies around as litter. Litter looks bad, it blocks up drains and can be dangerous to animals and people.

Landfill

Large amounts of rubbish are taken to holes in the ground called landfill sites.

Rubbish can take years to rot. As waste rots, poison leaks into the soil and poisonous gases escape into the air. These gases affect our climate by causing global warming. Landfill sites are also expensive to control and maintain.

Incinerators

Incinerators are big fires or furnaces where rubbish is burnt, sending smoke into the air and creating ash that has to be got rid of.

Not all this rubbish needs to go into landfill. Some of it could easily be recycled or reused.

Action!

Make a rubbish diary.
Record what goes into the bin at home and in your classroom under these headings:
- Glass
- Paper and card
- Plastic
- Food and garden waste
- Textiles
- Other.

Too much rubbish
Households, shops and factories all produce rubbish. Some rubbish, such as food and paper, is biodegradable. This means it breaks down naturally over time and disappears. Other rubbish, made of materials such as glass, metal and plastic, is non-biodegradable, which means it stays around for hundreds of years.

Challenge!

You can help.
- Reduce means to make less.
- Reduce the rubbish you throw away at home.
- Reduce the rubbish your class throws away at school.

Don't drop litter. Take it home with you or put it in the bin or recycling point.

7

Make less rubbish

To join the green team, one of the most useful things you can do is to reduce, or make less, rubbish in the first place. You can start at the shops.

Challenge!

Think before you buy something new.

Ask yourself:

Do I really need it?

Have I already got one?

Can I borrow one?

How many times will I use it?

Can I use something else instead?

How long will I be interested in it?

When you've answered all those questions, ask yourself, do I still want to buy it?

Throw away

People say we live in a 'throw-away society'. This means we use things and then throw them away, sometimes when they are still quite new. But you can change that. First of all, try not to buy so much!

Making a list helps you to buy exactly what you need. You won't buy too much food or things you don't need that you will throw away without even using.

Freecycle

Cut down on what you throw away. The Freecycle Network was founded in May 2003 in Tuscan, USA, to help save desert landscape from being taken over by landfill sites. Today, there are Freecycle groups all over the world. They try to keep usable things out of landfill sites by passing them on to someone who will use them. Their aim is to reduce the number of things we make and buy.

At this Freecycle event, everyone brought along stuff they didn't want and other people took it home and reused it.

Action!

Don't throw out usable things you don't want any more.

- Hold a sale and give the money you make to an environmental charity.
- Join an organisation such as Freecycle and give usable things away.

Pete **Jack**

Jack's feet will grow and his roller blades will soon be too small for him. He can borrow a pair from his older brother Pete, and pass his onto someone else when they are too small for him. That way, he will make less rubbish than if he buys a new pair.

Packaging and wrapping

Most of the rubbish we throw away is packaging. Reducing the amount of packaging we bring into our homes and schools will help to reduce the waste mountain.

Food is one of the most packaged things we buy. Packaging makes the food more expensive, and leads to more litter (above right).

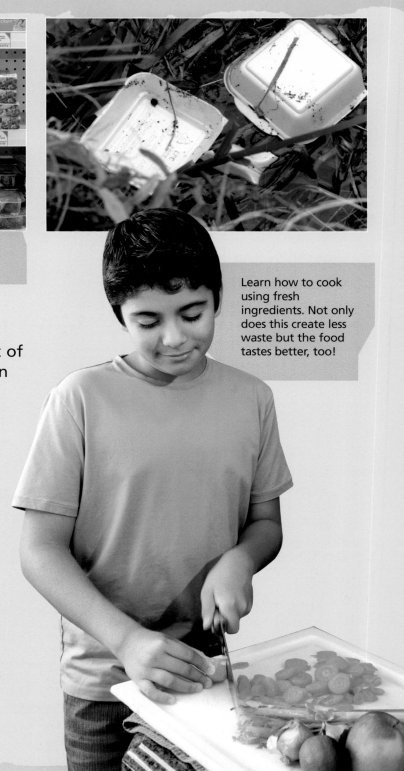

Learn how to cook using fresh ingredients. Not only does this create less waste but the food tastes better, too!

Food packaging

Food packaging helps to preserve, protect and keep food fresh. But a lot of the packaging is not necessary and can create litter that does not rot away.

Learn to cook

Ready-cooked meals come in lots of packaging. Cooking from fresh ingredients saves packaging and is usually a healthier choice.

School supplies

School supplies arrive in all kinds of packaging. Cardboard and paper are biodegradable and recyclable, but polystyrene balls and bubble wrap are not.

Challenge!

Make choices at the shops.

- Choose one big packet, carton or bottle instead of lots of smaller ones.
- Buy concentrated cleaning products which use less packaging.
- Don't buy products with several layers of packaging when one will do. If you do not think the packaging is necessary, challenge the shop about its packaging policy by writing a letter or talking to staff.

This girl is drawing on recycled paper, made from waste paper collected at her school.

Case study – Reusing packaging

The Gene Rosenfield "Preserve Our Environment Leadership" Award is awarded every year to an American student for his or her efforts in protecting the environment around them. Sara Merando from Lakeland Regional High School, Wanaque, conserved paper by reusing paper that other students discarded. She collected used paper from the copy room for her use as well. Sara was able to collect so much paper that she has not had to buy a notebook since her first year at high school.

Creative ideas

Other students at Sara's school reused their paper and packaging.

- Shredded paper was used to make more paper (see page 19) which was then made into scrapbooks.
- Photo frames, notepaper cubes and bags were just some of the other things the students made.

A strong bag made from recycled newspaper.

Books and magazines

When you have read a book, don't throw it away or leave it on a shelf getting dusty. There are all kinds of things you can do with books.

You don't have to buy a book to read it. You can borrow it from your local library.

Challenge!

Give old books a new life.
- Can you mend old or torn books?
- Can you lend books to friends?
- Can you sell books and use the money to buy more?
- Can you give your old books to schools or charities?

Libraries

Libraries are a great way of reusing books. If you aren't a member of your local library, join it now. Instead of buying a new book, you can borrow a selection and take them home to read. When you have finished, take the books back to the library and choose a new selection to read.

Oil

Oil is used to make the plastic used for bags. Reducing and reusing plastic bags will help to save oil, a precious natural resource.

 Plastic bags can choke and suffocate people as well as wildlife. Keep them away from young children. Make sure any you use are punctured with small holes to let in air.

Two swans fight over a plastic bag, mistaking it for food.

We depend on oil for fuel and to make plastic, but there is only a limited amount left.

Helping the environment

Reducing the number of plastic bags we use will help to keep the environment free of poisonous and dangerous litter. Plastic is a man-made material. It won't biodegrade like natural materials. Plastic bags break down into small, poisonous pieces that end up in the soil, the sea, rivers, sand and shingle where birds and fish accidentally eat them. Plastic bags floating in the sea look like jelly fish which are food to many sea animals. The animals eat the plastic bags and are poisoned, or choke on them.

 ## Action!

Use your old plastic bags to make one big, very strong bag.

• Ask an adult to help you cut plastic bags into strips. Use the strips to knit, crochet, weave or plait a new strong bag.

• Have a competition at school for the best reused plastic bag design.

• Buy a couple of textile shopping bags and remember to use them instead of asking for a plastic shopping bag.

  21

Disposables

Disposables are things we use and throw away such as nappies, felt-tip pens, paper plates and polystyrene cups. They are very easy for us to use but they can cause damage to the environment.

A plastic cup can be reused in all kinds of different ways. It makes a good flower pot. What other ways of reusing it can you think of?

Challenge!

Give up using disposables.

• Before you buy something, ask yourself how many times you will use it. If the answer is you will only use it once, don't buy it!

• If you do buy something that can only be used once, think of a way to reuse it, for example using plastic cups as plant pots.

Disposable nappies

You may have a baby brother or sister who uses disposable nappies. One of the raw materials that disposable nappies are made from is oil. Energy is also used to make them. These are used once, thrown away and sent to landfill sites where they take a very long time to break down. Persuade your parents only to buy reusable nappies.

Some towelling nappies can be washed and used again and again.

Make your pens last as long as possible. Put the tops back on to stop them drying out.

Don't use disposable cutlery for picnics. If you have to, try washing and reusing them afterwards.

Pens

Brightly coloured plastic pens are disposable. Once the ink has run out, you throw them away and they go to landfill. Buy refillable pens when you can.

Picnics

Paper and plastic plates, cups, knives, forks and spoons and wooden chopsticks are often used once and then thrown away. It saves on washing up, but harms the environment.

 ## Action!

Think when you pack a picnic or school lunch box.

- Don't use disposable wrapping, cups, plates, napkins or cutlery.
- Take the right amount of food and there will be nothing to throw away!

When you pack your school bag, think about what is in it. What can be reused, and what will have to be thrown away?

Toys

Toys help you to use your imagination and learn new things.
You can play with them by yourself or with friends. It is much better for the environment to make your own toys or reuse old ones. Making new toys and games uses up lots of energy and natural resources.

An old bicycle wheel makes a good hoop to bowl along.

Make your own games

Some of the best games need only your imagination. Others can be made from objects lying around the home, with no need to buy anything new. It is easy to make an Oware set like the one opposite. Use two egg boxes (for 6 eggs) to make a board of two rows of "cells". Then find 48 seeds or beans and put four in each cell. The object of the game is to capture more seeds than your opponent. To find out the rules of the game go to www. wikipedia.org/oware.

This is a traditional Owa. board and pieces. Make your o. from objects around the house.

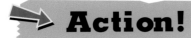

Are you playing with the toys you've already got?

- Have a clear-out of your toy box.
- Find a new home for toys that you only sometimes or never play with. Take them to a charity shop or to your school sale.
- You can give toys in good condition to a toy library.

Case study – A toy library

Rather than put your toys in a cupboard when you get bored with them, why not let someone else enjoy them? Lots of charities collect toys and games. UNRWA (the United Nations Relief and Works Agency for Palestine Refugees in the Near East) is setting up 11 toy libraries in the war-torn Gaza Strip in Israel to provide places where around 3,800 children will be able to enjoy playing safely. The centres will also create new opportunities for women, children and the disabled to join in with their local communities having fun together.

An UNRWA toy library full of second-hand toys ready for children to enjoy.

Batteries

Toys often need batteries to make them work. Batteries are packs of chemicals. When batteries are thrown away the chemicals can leak into the soil. Find out where batteries can be disposed of responsibly. Buy rechargeable batteries that can be reused again and again. Use solar-powered batteries, which are re-charged by sunlight.

Most electric toys use batteries. Opt for rechargeable rather than disposable ones.

Challenge!

Use your imagination.

Some toys can be played with again and again in all kinds of different ways. Try out these toys and games and discover that toys don't have to be expensive to be fun.

- Cards
- Oware/Mancala
- Skipping rope
- Football
- Kite
- Dressing-up box
- Marbles.

A green fair

You could organise your own green summer fair with a recycling theme. Invite the local community to share what you have learnt about what we can all do to save the planet.

Green team

One Junior School Green Team had lots of ideas for their stall. First they held a competition for the best object made from reused materials to be sold at the fair with prizes from a charity shop. They sold paper weights made from stones, driftwood signs, plants and flowers grown by the gardening club and shoe bags and aprons made from reused material.

Amber (4M):

"It was a good idea to get people to reuse their stuff to make stuff."

Emily (4M):

"Re-userific! I liked … seeing all the things people had made from re-usable things. I loved the dream-catcher made from an old piece of wool, corks and see-through plastic paper."

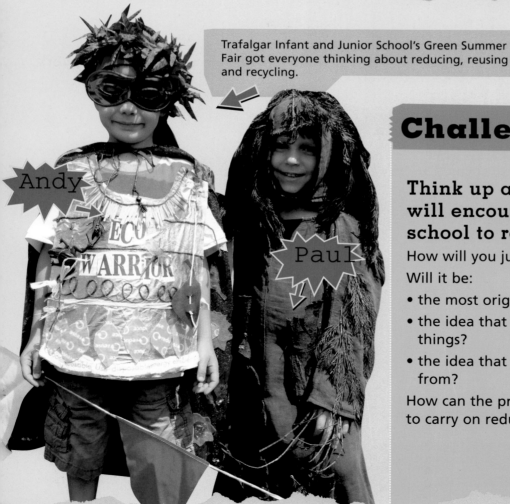

Trafalgar Infant and Junior School's Green Summer Fair got everyone thinking about reducing, reusing and recycling.

Andy

Paul

Challenge!

Think up a competition that will encourage everyone at school to reduce and reuse.

How will you judge the winning entry?

Will it be:

- the most original and imaginative idea?
- the idea that makes best use of reusing things?
- the idea that everyone learns the most from?

How can the prize encourage the winner to carry on reducing and reusing?

The House of the Future designs were displayed at the fair so other people could share what the children had learnt.

Displays, posters and leaflets helped visitors to the Recycle stall learn about how recycling helps protect the environment.

House of the Future Competition

A competition to design a house of the future got the children thinking about eco-friendly materials and waste and energy saving ideas. Some homes already have solar panels to heat water, and wind turbines to make electricity.

Food

The food and drink stalls were planned to create as little rubbish as possible. Lunches were sold in brown paper bags that were recycled on the spot. Drinks were served in strong plastic cups that could be washed and reused.

Organisations

Organisations concerned with green issues will usually work with schools to help them learn about saving the planet and taking action. At this green fair, the local council, Friends of the Earth, Fairtrade and the local Environment Network joined together to set up stalls so people could find out about the work they do and get involved.

Action!

Plan a green fair for your school.

• How will you encourage people to reduce waste and reuse things?

• What stalls will there be?

• What events will you have?

• What food will you serve and how will you serve it?

• Who will you invite?

• What do you hope everyone will learn?

• How do you hope people will change what they do?

27

Glossary

Biodegrade
When something biodegrades, it breaks down naturally and becomes part of the soil, water or air. Vegetable peelings biodegrade but most plastic does not.

Developing country
A developing country is one that is mostly poor but is developing its schools, hospitals, farming and industry.

Exchange
When you exchange things, you give something and get something back in return. At a uniform exchange, you give the uniform you have grown out of and exchange it for one that fits you.

Greenhouse gas
Gases such as carbon dioxide that contribute to global warming.

Global warming
A rise in the Earth's temperature caused mainly by burning oil, gas and coal.

Habitat
A place where an animal or plant lives.

Landfill
A way of getting rid of waste by burying it in the ground.

Natural resource
Something that is useful to people found in nature such as oil and wood.

Polluting
Something is polluting if it harms the natural environment such as air, soil or water. Exhaust fumes from cars pollute the air. Oil spills at sea pollute the water.

Raw material
A natural material that things are made from, such as cotton, oil and wood.

Recharge
To refill with energy. Rechargeable batteries can be refilled with energy when they run out and used again.

Reduce
Reduce means to make less. Reducing the waste we make helps to reduce the amount of rubbish going into landfill.

Reuse
Reuse means to use again. If we reuse plastic bags, for example, it reduces the number being made and sent to landfill.

Weblinks

www.freecycle.org
More than 4,000 groups of freecyclers across the globe give and get stuff for free, reusing and keeping good things out of landfill sites. Find a group to join near where you live.

www.bookaid.org
Find out how you can donate books and help to give children all over the world the chance to read and learn.

www.oxfam.org.uk/coolplanet/kidsweb/oxfam/action.htm
Take your clothes, toys and other reusable stuff to an Oxfam shop near you. Money raised will help people all over the world.

www.fomo.co.uk
Friends of Mulanje Orphans collect clothes and school uniforms to help children in Malawi go to school.

www.eco-shools.org.uk
Your school can become part of an international group of schools committed to caring for the environment.

www.computeraid.org
Instead of throwing usable computers away, find out how they can be reused by schools and businesses in Africa.

www.olliesworld.com
A website for children to learn to reduce, reuse and recycle.

Index